WORLD'S BIGGEST

FREAKY-BIG Airplanes

by Meish Goldish

Consultants:

Ned Allen, Editor in Chief, AIAA Library of Flight,
and Chief Scientist at Lockheed Martin's Skunk Works

Mike Geddry, Sr., President and Curator
of the Santa Maria Museum of Flight

BEARPORT
PUBLISHING

New York, New York

Credits

Cover and Title Page, © Zavodskov Anatoliy Nikolaevich/Shutterstock; TOC, © Denis Klimov/Shutterstock; 4, © Culver Pictures, Inc./SuperStock; 5T, © DPA/Landov; 5BL, © Jonathan Drake/Bloomberg News/ Landov; 5BR, © Marlene Awaad/Maxppp/Landov; 6, © Waltraud Grubitzsch/DPA/Newscom; 7, © Tim De Groot/AirTeamImages; 8, © Agence France Presse/Newscom; 9T, © MAI/Landov; 9B, © Cristina Quicler/ Agence France Presse/Newscom; 10L, © Christian Lantenois/Maxppp/Landov; 10R, © Kateryna Dyellalova/ Shutterstock; 11, © PhotoPQR/Le Courrier Picard/Fred Haslin/Newscom; 12, © Arne Dedert/DPA/Newscom; 13, © Roger Ressmeyer/Corbis; 14, © AP Images/Elaine Thompson; 15, © AP Images/Elaine Thompson; 16, Courtesy of NASA/Carla Thomas; 17, © Gary I Rothstein/epa/Corbis; 18, © Reuters/Landov; 19, © age fotostock/SuperStock; 20, © David Gowans/Alamy; 21, © AP Images/Reed Saxon; 22TL, © Randy Jolly/Aero Graphics, Inc./Corbis; 22TR, © Matt Stroshane/Getty Images; 22BL, © Alan Dep/San Jose Mercury News/ MCT/Landov; 23BR, Courtesy of ICO Global Communications/Space Systems Loral; 24A, © Stephen Strathdee/ Shutterstock; 24B, © Eric Gevaert/Shutterstock; 24C, © Renata Fedosova/Shutterstock; 24D, © Alperium/ Shutterstock; 24E, © Sebastian Kaulitzki/Shutterstock; 24F, © MAI/Landov; 24G, © foray/Shutterstock.

Publisher: Kenn Goin
Editorial Director: Adam Siegel
Creative Director: Spencer Brinker
Photo Researcher: Picture Perfect Professionals, LLC
Design: Debrah Kaiser

Library of Congress Cataloging-in-Publication Data

Goldish, Meish.
  Freaky-big airplanes / by Meish Goldish.
    p. cm. — (World's biggest)
  Includes bibliographical references and index.
  ISBN-13: 978-1-59716-959-2 (library binding)
  ISBN-10: 1-59716-959-5 (library binding)
  1. Transport planes—Juvenile literature. I. Title.

  TL685.7.G65 2010
  629.13—dc22

                    2009014620

For more information, write to Bearport Publishing Company, Inc., 101 Fifth Avenue, Suite 6R, New York, New York 10003. Printed in the United States of America.

10 9 8 7 6 5 4 3 2 1

CONTENTS

AIRBUS A380

Length: 239 feet, 3 inches (72.9 m) **Height:** 79 feet, 7 inches (24.3 m)

Wingspan: 261 feet, 8 inches (79.8 m) **Maximum Takeoff Weight:**
1,235,000 pounds (560,187 kg)

In 1903, two brothers, Orville and Wilbur Wright, built the first engine-powered airplane that could fly. The *Wright Flyer* stayed in the air for 12 seconds on its first flight and traveled 120 feet (37 m). The plane held just one person— Orville Wright, the pilot.

Today's airplanes fly much farther and for a much longer time. They also hold many more people. The Airbus A380 is the biggest **passenger plane** in the world. It can hold up to 840 travelers. This plane isn't just big—it's freaky big! Its **wingspan** is so wide that the *Wright Flyer* could have taken off and landed on the A380's wings!

The *Wright Flyer* taking
its first flight

Orville Wright did not sit in the *Wright Flyer* as it flew. Instead, he lay flat on the lower wing in the middle of the plane.

ANTONOV An-225

Length: 275 feet, 7 inches (84 m)   **Height:** 59 feet, 9 inches (18.2 m)

Wingspan: 290 feet (88.4 m)   **Maximum Takeoff Weight:**
1,322,750 pounds (599,989 kg)

Although the Airbus A380 is huge, it isn't the world's biggest **aircraft**. That record is held by the Antonov An-225. Made by the Soviet Union, the An-225 is the largest airplane ever built. It doesn't carry passengers, however. It's a **transport plane** that flies **cargo** to different places around the world.

The An-225 was first used to carry large equipment for the Soviet space program. Today, the plane flies other kinds of oversize—and heavy—cargo. It can carry a load of more than 550,000 pounds (249,476 kg). That's like having 40 big elephants on board!

UR-82060

The Antonov An-225 is almost as long as a football field.

Inside the An-225,
where cargo is stored

INTERNATIONAL CARGO
TRANSPORTER
Phone: +38(044)443-00-18
Fax: +38(044)454-28-52
E-mail: office@antonov.kiev.ua

STAGE ⊟   STAGE ⊟   STAGE ⊟

ANTONOV 225

C-5 GALAXY

Length: 247 feet, 10 inches (75.5 m)   **Height:** 65 feet, 1 inch (19.8 m)

Wingspan: 222 feet, 9 inches (67.9 m)   **Maximum Takeoff Weight:**
840,000 pounds (381,018 kg)

Transport planes carry many kinds of cargo. The C-5 Galaxy flies tanks and other military equipment around the world. The plane is used by the U.S. Air Force. When it was first built in the late 1960s, the C-5 was the world's largest airplane. Today it is still one of the biggest.

The C-5 Galaxy is used in times of war. The plane is large enough to hold army trucks, helicopters, or small planes. The giant aircraft can fly long distances at a moment's notice to deliver its goods.

The C-5 Galaxy carries soldiers along with its military cargo.

AIR FORCE RESERVE COMMAND

A helicopter being loaded onto the C-5 Galaxy

The C-5 Galaxy speeds through the air at 518 miles per hour (834 kph).

AIRBUS BELUGA

Length: 184 feet, 3 inches (56.2 m) **Height:** 56 feet, 7 inches (17.2 m)

Wingspan: 147 feet, 2 inches (44.9 m) **Maximum Takeoff Weight:** 341,713 pounds (154,998 kg)

Because airplanes are so big, some people have called them "flying whales." One kind of airplane is even named after a whale. It's the Airbus Beluga (buh-LOO-guh). This transport plane is shaped like a beluga whale. The unusual design makes it possible for extra-large cargo to be stored on board.

The Beluga has more space to hold cargo than other large transport planes, such as the C-5 Galaxy. However, the Beluga can't carry as much weight. The Beluga can hold 103,617 pounds (47,000 kg) while the C-5 Galaxy can carry cargo weighing more than twice that—up to 270,000 pounds (122,470 kg)!

A beluga whale

The Airbus Beluga was originally called the Super Transporter. The nickname "Beluga" grew so popular, however, that it's now the official name of the airplane.

BOEING 747-400

Length: 231 feet, 10 inches (70.7 m)   **Height:** 63 feet, 8 inches (19.4 m)

Wingspan: 211 feet, 5 inches (64.4 m)   **Maximum Takeoff Weight:**
875,000 pounds (396,893 kg)

Which airplane is nicknamed the "jumbo jet"? It's the Boeing 747-400. This giant aircraft can hold 420 travelers. When it took its first flight in 1988, the Boeing 747-400 was the world's biggest passenger plane. It held the record for almost 20 years until the Airbus A380 came along in 2005.

Today, the Boeing 747-400 is still a very popular plane. More than 60 different airlines use it. Passengers love how roomy—and fast—it is. Flying through the air at speeds of up to 614 miles per hour (988 kph), the Boeing 747-400 is the world's fastest passenger plane used by airlines.

The tail of the Boeing 747-400 is taller than a six-story building.

BOEING DREAMLIFTER

Length: 235 feet, 2 inches (71.7 m)   **Height:** 70 feet, 8 inches (21.5 m)

Wingspan: 211 feet, 5 inches (64.4 m)   **Maximum Takeoff Weight:**
803,000 pounds (364,235 kg)

The Boeing Company makes more than just big passenger planes. It also builds huge transport planes. Its largest is called the Dreamlifter, which is a longer and taller version of its 747-400 passenger plane.

The Dreamlifter is used to carry large airplane parts that Boeing buys from places around the world. The Dreamlifter then delivers the parts to the United States, where they are put together at a factory in Everett, Washington.

Boeing decided to build the Dreamlifter because shipping airplane parts across the ocean by boat is too slow. It can take ships up to 30 days to deliver the parts. Using the Dreamlifter can take as little as one!

DREAM)LIFTER

The rear section of the Boeing Dreamlifter is able to swing open in order to take on extra-large cargo.

SHUTTLE CARRIER AIRCRAFT

Length: 231 feet, 10 inches (70.7 m)

Wingspan: 195 feet, 8 inches (59.6 m)

Height: 63 feet, 5 inches (19.3 m)

Maximum Takeoff Weight: 713,000 pounds (323,411 kg)

Some big transport planes carry smaller planes inside them. The Shuttle Carrier Aircraft works differently. It carries a **space shuttle orbiter** on its back!

The Shuttle Carrier Aircraft is part of the U.S. space program. After a space shuttle orbiter returns to Earth, the carrier flies it from the place where it landed to the Kennedy Space Center in Florida. Scientists call the Shuttle Carrier Aircraft by a shorter name, SCA—but that's the only short thing about this freaky-big plane!

space shuttle orbiter

Shuttle Carrier Aircraft

space shuttle orbiter

Shuttle Carrier Aircraft

A space shuttle orbiter weighs around 171,000 pounds (77,564 kg). As a result, a Shuttle Carrier Aircraft uses twice as much fuel to stay up in the air when it is flying with such a heavy vehicle on its back.

B-52 BOMBER

Length: 159 feet, 4 inches (48.6 m)   **Height:** 40 feet, 8 inches (12.4 m)

Wingspan: 185 feet (56.4 m)   **Maximum Takeoff Weight:**
488,000 pounds (221,353 kg)

During wartime, countries often use planes to drop bombs. One of the biggest types of bombers is the B-52 Stratofortress. It can carry up to 70,000 pounds (31,751 kg) of bombs on board. It can also fly farther than any other bomber without having to refuel.

The U.S. Air Force has been flying B-52s for more than 50 years. In addition to dropping bombs, the war planes can also launch cruise missiles. Usually five crew members are on board a B-52 as it zooms through the air at up to 650 miles per hour (1,046 kph). Even while moving at high speeds, these planes are able to hit their targets.

A B-52 dropping bombs

During the Gulf War in 1991, seven B-52s took off from an Air Force base in Louisiana, flew to Iraq where they launched cruise missiles, and returned to Louisiana without stopping in just 35 hours. At the time, it was the longest air strike in history.

WATER BOMBER

Length: 117 feet, 3 inches (35.7 m)   **Height:** 38 feet, 5 inches (11.7 m)

Wingspan: 200 feet (61 m)   **Maximum Takeoff Weight:** 165,000 pounds (74,843 kg)

Some planes are called bombers, yet they don't drop bombs. Water bombers are used to fight fires. They drop water on flames that have spread out of control on the ground.

One type of water bomber is the flying boat. It flies low over a lake or ocean and scoops up water. Then it soars into the sky and drops its wet load on the fire below.

A water bomber can scoop up 7,200 gallons (27,255 l) of water in about 25 seconds. Today engineers are designing new water bombers that will have even larger tanks. How big will these and other airplanes get? The sky's the limit!

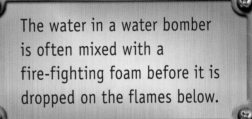

The water in a water bomber is often mixed with a fire-fighting foam before it is dropped on the flames below.

MORE BIG AIRCRAFT

Airplanes aren't the only big machines flying
through the sky. Here are four others.

At about 99 feet (30 m) long, the
Sikorsky CH-53E Super Stallion is the
biggest helicopter used by the U.S.
military. It can lift more than 30,000
pounds (13,608 kg) and carry up to
55 soldiers.

Standing more than 230 feet (70 m)
tall, the Boeing Delta 4-Heavy is one
of the biggest unmanned rockets
in the world. As tall as a 23-story
building, this giant rocket delivers
satellites into space.

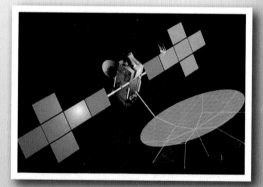

Stretching 246 feet (75 m) long,
the world's biggest airship is the
Airship Ventures Zeppelin. It offers
tours over the San Francisco Bay
area in California.

The world's biggest commercial satellite
is the ICO G1. More than 100 feet
(30 m) wide, this giant satellite orbits
in space, relaying television signals and
other communication services to Earth.

GLOSSARY

aircraft (AIR-kraft) any vehicle that can fly

cargo (KAR-goh) items that are delivered by plane, truck, or ship

passenger plane (PASS-uhn-jur PLAYN) an airplane that flies travelers from one place to another

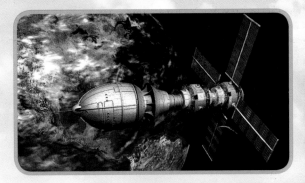

satellites (SAT-uh-*lites*) spacecraft that are sent into orbit in space in order to send information back to Earth

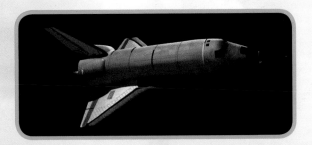

space shuttle orbiter (SPAYSS SHUHT-uhl OR-bit-ur) a reusable spacecraft that carries people, supplies, and equipment into space

transport plane (TRANSS-port PLAYN) an airplane used to fly items from one place to another

wingspan (WING-span) the distance between the tips of an airplane's wings

INDEX

BIBLIOGRAPHY

Endres, Günter. *Major Airlines of the World.* Shrewsbury, England: Airlife Publishing (2002).

Haenggi, Michael. *Boeing Widebodies.* St. Paul, MN: Motorbooks International (2003).

Norris, Guy, and Mark Wagner. *Giant Jetliners.* Osceola, WI: MBI Publishing (1997).

Spenser, Jay. *The Airplane: How Ideas Gave Us Wings.* New York: HarperCollins (2008).

READ MORE

Bingham, Caroline. *Airplane.* New York: DK Publishing (2003).

Masters, Nancy Robinson. *The Airplane (Inventions That Shaped the World).* New York: Franklin Watts (2004).

Millard, Anne. *DK Big Book of Airplanes.* New York: DK Publishing (2001).

LEARN MORE ONLINE

To learn more about freaky-big airplanes, visit
www.bearportpublishing.com/WorldsBiggest.com

ABOUT THE AUTHOR

Meish Goldish has written more than 200 books for children. He lives in Brooklyn, New York.